ZARATHUSTRA'S
DISCOURSES

FRIEDRICH NIETZSCHE

ZARATHUSTRA'S
DISCOURSES

TRANSLATED BY R. J. HOLLINGDALE

PENGUIN BOOKS

PENGUIN BOOKS

Published by the Penguin Group

Penguin Books USA Inc., 375 Hudson Street,
New York, New York 10014, U.S.A.
Penguin Books Ltd, 27 Wrights Lane,
London W8 5TZ, England
Penguin Books Australia Ltd, Ringwood,
Victoria, Australia
Penguin Books Canada Ltd, 10 Alcorn Avenue,
Toronto, Ontario, Canada M4V 3B2
Penguin Books (N.Z.) Ltd, 182–190 Wairau Road,
Auckland 10, New Zealand

Penguin Books Ltd, Registered Offices:
Harmondsworth, Middlesex, England

Published in Penguin Books 1995

Translation copyright © R. J. Hollingdale, 1961
All rights reserved

This extract is from *Thus Spoke Zarathustra*, translated by
R. J. Hollingdale, published by Penguin Books.

ISBN 0 14 60.0175 3

Printed in the United States of America

Except in the United States of America, this book is sold subject
to the condition that it shall not, by way of trade or otherwise, be
lent, re-sold, hired out, or otherwise circulated without the pub-
lisher's prior consent in any form of binding or cover other than
that in which it is published and without a similar condition in-
cluding this condition being imposed on the subsequent pur-
chaser.

CONTENTS

Prologue

WHEN Zarathustra was thirty years old, he left his home and the lake of his home and went into the mountains. Here he had the enjoyment of his spirit and his solitude and he did not weary of it for ten years. But at last his heart turned – and one morning he rose with the dawn, stepped before the sun, and spoke to it thus:

Great star! What would your happiness be, if you had not those for whom you shine!

You have come up here to my cave for ten years: you would have grown weary of your light and of this journey, without me, my eagle and my serpent.

But we waited for you every morning, took from you your superfluity and blessed you for it.

Behold! I am weary of my wisdom, like a bee that has gathered too much honey; I need hands outstretched to take it.

I should like to give it away and distribute it, until the wise among men have again become happy in their folly and the poor happy in their wealth.

To that end, I must descend into the depths: as you do at evening, when you go behind the sea and bring light to the underworld too, superabundant star!

Like you, I must *go down* – as men, to whom I want to descend, call it.

So bless me then, tranquil eye, that can behold without envy even an excessive happiness!

Bless the cup that wants to overflow, that the waters may flow golden from him and bear the reflection of your joy over all the world!

Behold! This cup wants to be empty again, and Zarathustra wants to be man again.

Thus began Zarathustra's down-going.

2

Zarathustra went down the mountain alone, and no one met him. But when he entered the forest, an old man, who had left his holy hut to look for roots in the forest, suddenly stood before him. And the old man spoke thus to Zarathustra:

'This wanderer is no stranger to me: he passed by here many years ago. He was called Zarathustra; but he has changed.

'Then you carried your ashes to the mountains: will you today carry your fire into the valleys? Do you not fear an incendiary's punishment?

'Yes, I recognize Zarathustra. His eyes are clear, and no disgust lurks about his mouth. Does he not go along like a dancer?

'How changed Zarathustra is! Zarathustra has become – a child, an awakened-one: what do you want now with the sleepers?

'You lived in solitude as in the sea, and the sea bore you. Alas, do you want to go ashore? Alas, do you want again to drag your body yourself?'

Zarathustra answered: 'I love mankind.'

'Why', said the saint, 'did I go into the forest and the desert? Was it not because I loved mankind all too much?

'Now I love God: mankind I do not love. Man is too imperfect a thing for me. Love of mankind would destroy me.'

Zarathustra answered: 'What did I say of love? I am bringing mankind a gift.'

'Give them nothing,' said the saint. 'Rather take something off them and bear it with them – that will please them best; if only it be pleasing to you!

'And if you want to give to them, give no more than an alms, and let them beg for that!'

'No,' answered Zarathustra, 'I give no alms. I am not poor enough for that.'

The saint laughed at Zarathustra, and spoke thus: 'See to it that they accept your treasures! They are mistrustful of hermits, and do not believe that we come to give.

'Our steps ring too lonely through their streets. And when at night they hear in their beds a man going by long before the sun has risen, they probably ask themselves: Where is that thief going?

'Do not go to men, but stay in the forest! Go rather to the animals! Why will you not be as I am – a bear among bears, a bird among animals?'

'And what does the saint do in the forest?' asked Zarathustra.

The saint answered: 'I make songs and sing them, and when I make songs, I laugh, weep, and mutter: thus I praise God.

'With singing, weeping, laughing, and muttering I praise the God who is my God. But what do you bring us as a gift?'

When Zarathustra heard these words, he saluted the saint and said: 'What should I have to give you! But let me go quickly, that I may take nothing from you!' And thus they parted from one another, the old man and Zarathustra, laughing as two boys laugh.

But when Zarathustra was alone, he spoke thus to his heart: 'Could it be possible! This old saint has not yet heard in his forest that *God is dead*!'

3

When Zarathustra arrived at the nearest of the towns lying against the forest, he found in that very place many people assembled in the market square: for it had been announced that a tight-rope walker would be appearing. And Zarathustra spoke thus to the people:

I teach you the Superman. Man is something that should be overcome. What have you done to overcome him?

All creatures hitherto have created something beyond themselves: and do you want to be the ebb of this great tide, and return to the animals rather than overcome man?

What is the ape to men? A laughing-stock or a painfu

embarrassment. And just so shall man be to the Superman: a laughing-stock or a painful embarrassment.

You have made your way from worm to man, and much in you is still worm. Once you were apes, and even now man is more of an ape than any ape.

But he who is the wisest among you, he also is only a discord and hybrid of plant and of ghost. But do I bid you become ghosts or plants?

Behold, I teach you the Superman.

The Superman is the meaning of the earth. Let your will say: The Superman *shall be* the meaning of the earth!

I entreat you, my brothers, *remain true to the earth*, and do not believe those who speak to you of superterrestrial hopes! They are poisoners, whether they know it or not.

They are despisers of life, atrophying and self-poisoned men, of whom the earth is weary: so let them be gone!

Once blasphemy against God was the greatest blasphemy, but God died, and thereupon these blasphemers died too. To blaspheme the earth is now the most dreadful offence, and to esteem the bowels of the Inscrutable more highly than the meaning of the earth.

Once the soul looked contemptuously upon the body: and then this contempt was the supreme good – the soul wanted the body lean, monstrous, famished. So the soul thought to escape from the body and from the earth.

Oh, this soul was itself lean, monstrous, and famished: and cruelty was the delight of this soul!

But tell me, my brothers: What does your body say about your soul? Is your soul not poverty and dirt and a miserable ease?

In truth, man is a polluted river. One must be a sea, to receive a polluted river and not be defiled.

Behold, I teach you the Superman: he is this sea, in him your great contempt can go under.

What is the greatest thing you can experience? It is the hour of the great contempt. The hour in which even your happiness grows loathsome to you, and your reason and your virtue also.

The hour when you say: 'What good is my happiness? It is poverty and dirt and a miserable ease. But my happiness should justify existence itself!'

The hour when you say: 'What good is my reason? Does it long for knowledge as the lion for its food? It is poverty and dirt and a miserable ease!'

The hour when you say: 'What good is my virtue? It has not yet driven me mad! How tired I am of my good and my evil! It is all poverty and dirt and a miserable ease!'

The hour when you say: 'What good is my justice? I do not see that I am fire and hot coals. But the just man is fire and hot coals!'

The hour when you say: 'What good is my pity? Is not pity the cross upon which he who loves man is nailed? But my pity is no crucifixion!'

Have you ever spoken thus? Have you ever cried thus? Ah, that I had heard you crying thus!

It is not your sin, but your moderation that cries to heaven, your very meanness in sinning cries to heaven!

Where is the lightning to lick you with its tongue? Where is the madness, with which you should be cleansed?

Behold, I teach you the Superman: he is this lightning, he is this madness!

When Zarathustra had spoken thus, one of the people cried: 'Now we have heard enough of the tight-rope walker; let us see him, too!' And all the people laughed at Zarathustra. But the tight-rope walker, who thought that the words applied to him, set to work.

4

But Zarathustra looked at the people and marvelled. Then he spoke thus:

Man is a rope, fastened between animal and Superman – a rope over an abyss.

A dangerous going-across, a dangerous wayfaring, a dangerous looking-back, a dangerous shuddering and staying-still.

What is great in man is that he is a bridge and not a goal; what can be loved in man is that he is a *going-across* and a *down-going*.

I love those who do not know how to live except their lives be a down-going, for they are those who are going across

I love the great despisers, for they are the greatest venerators and arrows of longing for the other bank.

I love those who do not first seek beyond the stars for reasons to go down and to be sacrifices: but who sacrifice themselves to the earth, that the earth may one day belong to the Superman.

I love him who lives for knowledge and who wants knowledge that one day the Superman may live. And thus he wills his own downfall.

I love him who works and invents that he may build a house for the Superman and prepare earth, animals, and plants for him: for thus he wills his own downfall.

I love him who loves his virtue: for virtue is will to downfall and an arrow of longing.

I love him who keeps back no drop of spirit for himself, but wants to be the spirit of his virtue entirely: thus he steps as spirit over the bridge.

I love him who makes a predilection and a fate of his virtue: thus for his virtue's sake he will live or not live.

I love him who does not want too many virtues. One virtue is more virtue than two, because it is more of a knot for fate to cling to.

I love him whose soul is lavish, who neither wants nor returns thanks: for he always gives and will not preserve himself.

I love him who is ashamed when the dice fall in his favour and who then asks: Am I then a cheat? – for he wants to perish.

I love him who throws golden words in advance of his deeds and always performs more than he promised: for he wills his own downfall.

I love him who justifies the men of the future and redeems the men of the past: for he wants to perish by the men of the present.

I love him who chastises his God because he loves his God: for he must perish by the anger of his God.

I love him whose soul is deep even in its ability to be wounded, and whom even a little thing can destroy: thus he is glad to go over the bridge.

I love him whose soul is overfull, so that he forgets himself and all things are in him: thus all things become his downfall.

I love him who is of a free spirit and a free heart: thus his head is only the bowels of his heart, but his heart drives him to his downfall.

I love all those who are like heavy drops falling singly from the dark cloud that hangs over mankind: they prophesy the coming of the lightning and as prophets they perish.

Behold, I am a prophet of the lightning and a heavy drop from the cloud: but this lightning is called *Superman*.

5

When Zarathustra had spoken these words he looked again at the people and fell silent. There they stand (he said to his heart), there they laugh: they do not understand me, I am not the mouth for these ears.

Must one first shatter their ears to teach them to hear with their eyes? Must one rumble like drums and Lenten preachers? Or do they believe only those who stammer?

They have something of which they are proud. What is it called that makes them proud? They call it culture, it distinguishes them from the goatherds.

Therefore they dislike hearing the word 'contempt' spoken of them. So I shall speak to their pride.

So I shall speak to them of the most contemptible man: and that is the *Ultimate Man*.

And thus spoke Zarathustra to the people:

It is time for man to fix his goal. It is time to plant the seed of his highest hope.

His soil is still rich enough for it. But this soil will one day be poor and weak; no longer will a high tree be able to grow from it.

Alas! The time is coming when man will no more shoot the arrow of his longing out over mankind, and the string of his bow will have forgotten how to twang!

I tell you: one must have chaos in one, to give birth to a dancing star. I tell you: you still have chaos in you.

Alas! The time is coming when man will give birth to no more stars. Alas! The time of the most contemptible man is coming, the man who can no longer despise himself.

Behold! I shall show you the *Ultimate Man*.

'What is love? What is creation? What is longing? What is a star?' thus asks the Ultimate Man and blinks.

The earth has become small, and upon it hops the Ultimate Man, who makes everything small. His race is as inexterminable as the flea; the Ultimate Man lives longest.

'We have discovered happiness,' say the Ultimate Men and blink.

They have left the places where living was hard: for one needs warmth. One still loves one's neighbour and rubs oneself against him: for one needs warmth.

Sickness and mistrust count as sins with them: one should go about warily. He is a fool who still stumbles over stones or over men!

A little poison now and then: that produces pleasant dreams. And a lot of poison at last, for a pleasant death.

They still work, for work is entertainment. But they take care the entertainment does not exhaust them.

Nobody grows rich or poor any more: both are too much of a burden. Who still wants to rule? Who obey? Both are too much of a burden.

No herdsman and one herd. Everyone wants the same thing, everyone is the same: whoever thinks otherwise goes voluntarily into the madhouse.

'Formerly all the world was mad,' say the most acute of them and blink.

They are clever and know everything that has ever happened: so there is no end to their mockery. They still quarrel, but they soon make up – otherwise indigestion would result.

They have their little pleasure for the day and their little pleasure for the night: but they respect health.

'We have discovered happiness,' say the Ultimate Men and blink.

And here ended Zarathustra's first discourse, which is also called 'The Prologue': for at this point the shouting and mirth of the crowd interrupted him. 'Give us this Ultimate Man, O Zarathustra' – so they cried – 'make us into this Ultimate Man! You can have the Superman!' And all the people laughed and shouted. But Zarathustra grew sad and said to his heart:

They do not understand me: I am not the mouth for these ears.

Perhaps I lived too long in the mountains, listened too much to the trees and the streams: now I speak to them as to goatherds.

Unmoved is my soul and bright as the mountains in the morning. But they think me cold and a mocker with fearful jokes.

And now they look at me and laugh: and laughing, they still hate me. There is ice in their laughter.

6

But then something happened that silenced every mouth and fixed every eye. In the meantime, of course, the tight-rope walker had begun his work: he had emerged from a little door and was proceeding across the rope, which was stretched between two towers and thus hung over the people and the market square. Just as he had reached the middle of his course the little door opened again and a brightly-dressed fellow like a buffoon sprang out and followed the former with rapid steps. 'Forward, lame-foot!' cried his fearsome voice, 'forward sluggard, intruder, pallid-face! Lest I tickle you with my heels! What are you doing here between towers? You belong in the tower, you should be locked up, you are blocking the way of a better man than you!' And with each word he came nearer and nearer to him: but when he was only a single pace behind him, there occurred the dreadful thing that silenced every mouth and fixed every eye: he emitted a cry like a devil and sprang over the man standing in his path. But the latter, when he saw his rival thus triumph, lost his head and the rope; he threw away his pole and fell, faster even than it, like a vortex of legs and arms. The market square and the people were like a sea in a storm: they flew apart in disorder, especially where the body would come crashing down.

But Zarathustra remained still and the body fell quite close to him, badly injured and broken but not yet dead. After a while, consciousness returned to the shattered man and he saw Zarathustra kneeling beside him. 'What are you doing?' he asked at length. 'I've known for a long time that the Devil would trip me up. Now he's dragging me to Hell: are you trying to prevent him?'

'On my honour, friend,' answered Zarathustra, 'all you have spoken of does not exist: there is no Devil and no Hell. Your soul will be dead even before your body: therefore fear nothing any more!'

The man looked up mistrustfully. 'If you are speaking the truth,' he said then, 'I leave nothing when I leave life. I am not much more than an animal which has been taught to dance by blows and starvation.'

'Not so,' said Zarathustra. 'You have made danger your calling, there is nothing in that to despise. Now you perish through your calling: so I will bury you with my own hands.'

When Zarathustra had said this the dying man replied no more; but he motioned with his hand, as if he sought Zarathustra's hand to thank him.

In the meanwhile, evening had come and the market square was hidden in darkness: then the people dispersed, for even curiosity and terror grow tired. But Zarathustra sat on the ground beside the dead man and was sunk in thought: thus he forgot the time. But at length it became night and a cold wind blew over the solitary figure. Then Zarathustra arose and said to his heart:

Truly Zarathustra has had a handsome catch today! He caught no man, but he did catch a corpse.

Uncanny is human existence and still without meaning: a buffoon can be fatal to it.

I want to teach men the meaning of their existence: which is the Superman, the lightning from the dark cloud man.

But I am still distant from them, and my meaning does not speak to their minds. To men, I am still a cross between a fool and a corpse.

Dark is the night, dark are Zarathustra's ways. Come, cold and stiff companion! I am going to carry you to the place where I shall bury you with my own hands.

When Zarathustra had said this to his heart he loaded the corpse on to his back and set forth. He had got a hundred paces when a man crept up to him and whispered in his ear – and behold! it was the buffoon of the tower who spoke to him. 'Go away from this town, O Zarathustra,' he said. 'Too many here hate you. The good and the just hate you and call you their enemy and despiser; the faithful of the true faith hate you, and they call you a danger to the people. It was lucky for you that they laughed at you: and truly you spoke like a buffoon. It was lucky for you that you made company with the dead dog; by so abasing yourself you have saved yourself for today. But leave this town – or tomorrow I shall jump over you, a living man over a dead one.' And when he had said this, the man disappeared; Zarathustra, however, went on through the dark streets.

At the town gate the gravediggers accosted him: they shone their torch in his face, recognized Zarathustra and greatly derided him. 'Zarathustra is carrying the dead dog away: excellent that Zarathustra has become a gravedigger! For our hands are too clean for the roast. Does Zarathustra want to rob the Devil of his morsel? Good luck then! A hearty appetite! But if the Devil is a better thief than Zarathustra! – he will steal them both, he will eat them both!' And they laughed and put their heads together.

Zarathustra said nothing and went his way. When he had

walked for two hours past woods and swamps he had heard too much hungry howling of wolves and he grew hungry himself. So he stopped at a lonely house in which a light was burning.

'Hunger has waylaid me', said Zarathustra, 'like a robber. My hunger has waylaid me in woods and swamps, and in the depth of night.

'My hunger has astonishing moods. Often it comes to me only after mealtimes, and today it did not come at all: where has it been?'

And with that, Zarathustra knocked on the door of the house. An old man appeared; he carried a light and asked: 'Who comes here to me and to my uneasy sleep?'

'A living man and a dead,' said Zarathustra. 'Give me food and drink, I forgot about them during the day. He who feeds the hungry refreshes his own soul: thus speaks wisdom.'

The old man went away, but returned at once and offered Zarathustra bread and wine. 'This is a bad country for hungry people,' he said. 'That is why I live here. Animals and men come here to me, the hermit. But bid your companion eat and drink, he is wearier than you.' Zarathustra answered: 'My companion is dead, I shall hardly be able to persuade him.' 'That is nothing to do with me,' said the old man morosely. 'Whoever knocks at my door must take what I offer him. Eat, and fare you well!'

After that, Zarathustra walked two hours more and trusted to the road and to the light of the stars: for he was used to walking abroad at night and liked to look into the face of all that slept. But when morning dawned, Zarathustra found himself in a thick forest and the road disappeared. Then he laid the dead man in a hollow tree at his head – for he wanted to protect him from the wolves – and laid himself down on the mossy ground. And straightway fell asleep, weary in body but with a soul at rest.

9

Zarathustra slept long, and not only the dawn but the morning too passed over his head. But at length he opened his eyes: in surprise Zarathustra gazed into the forest and the stillness, in surprise he gazed into himself. Then he arose quickly, like a seafarer who suddenly sees land, and rejoiced: for he beheld a new truth. And then he spoke to his heart thus:

A light has dawned for me: I need companions, living ones, not dead companions and corpses which I carry with me wherever I wish.

But I need living companions who follow me because they want to follow themselves – and who want to go where I want to go.

A light has dawned for me: Zarathustra shall not speak to the people but to companions! Zarathustra shall not be herdsman and dog to the herd!

To lure many away from the herd – that is why I have come. The people and the herd shall be angry with me: the herdsmen shall call Zarathustra a robber.

I say herdsmen, but they call themselves the good and the

just. I say herdsmen: but they call themselves the faithful of the true faith.

Behold the good and the just! Whom do they hate most? Him who smashes their tables of values, the breaker, the law-breaker – but he is the creator.

Behold the faithful of all faiths! Whom do they hate the most? Him who smashes their tables of values, the breaker, the law-breaker – but he is the creator.

The creator seeks companions, not corpses or herds or believers. The creator seeks fellow-creators, those who inscribe new values on new tables.

The creator seeks companions and fellow-harvesters: for with him everything is ripe for harvesting. But he lacks his hundred sickles: so he tears off the ears of corn and is vexed.

The creator seeks companions and such as know how to whet their sickles. They will be called destroyers and despisers of good and evil. But they are harvesters and rejoicers.

Zarathustra seeks fellow-creators, fellow-harvesters, and fellow-rejoicers: what has he to do with herds and herdsmen and corpses?

And you, my first companion, fare you well! I have buried you well in your hollow tree, I have hidden you well from the wolves.

But I am leaving you, the time has come. Between dawn and dawn a new truth has come to me.

I will not be herdsman or gravedigger. I will not speak again to the people: I have spoken to a dead man for the last time.

I will make company with creators, with harvesters, with rejoicers: I will show them the rainbow and the stairway to the Superman.

I shall sing my song to the lone hermit and to the hermits in pairs; and I will make the heart of him who still has ears for unheard-of things heavy with my happiness.

I make for my goal, I go my way; I shall leap over the hesitating and the indolent. Thus may my going-forward be their going-down!

10

Zarathustra said this to his heart as the sun stood at noon: then he looked inquiringly into the sky – for he heard above him the sharp cry of a bird. And behold! An eagle was sweeping through the air in wide circles, and from it was hanging a serpent, not like a prey but like a friend: it was coiled around the eagle's neck.

'It is my animals!' said Zarathustra and rejoiced in his heart.

'The proudest animal under the sun and the wisest animal under the sun – they have come scouting.

'They wanted to learn if Zarathustra was still alive. Am I in fact alive?

'I found it more dangerous among men than among animals; Zarathustra is following dangerous paths. May my animals lead me!'

When Zarathustra had said this he recalled the words of the saint in the forest, sighed, and spoke thus to his heart:

'I wish I were wise! I wish I were wise from the heart of me, like my serpent!

'But I am asking the impossible: therefore I ask my pride always to go along with my wisdom!

'And if one day my wisdom should desert me – ah, it loves to fly away! – then may my pride too fly with my folly!'

Thus began Zarathustra's down-going.

Zarathustra's Discourses

OF THE THREE METAMORPHOSES

I NAME you three metamorphoses of the spirit: how the spirit shall become a camel, and the camel a lion, and the lion at last a child.

There are many heavy things for the spirit, for the strong, weight-bearing spirit in which dwell respect and awe: its strength longs for the heavy, for the heaviest.

What is heavy? thus asks the weight-bearing spirit, thus it kneels down like the camel and wants to be well laden.

What is the heaviest thing, you heroes? so asks the weight-bearing spirit, that I may take it upon me and rejoice in my strength.

Is it not this: to debase yourself in order to injure your pride? To let your folly shine out in order to mock your wisdom?

Or is it this: to desert our cause when it is celebrating its victory? To climb high mountains in order to tempt the tempter?

Or is it this: to feed upon the acorns and grass of knowledge and for the sake of truth to suffer hunger of the soul?

Or is it this: to be sick and to send away comforters and make friends with the deaf, who never hear what you ask?

Or is it this: to wade into dirty water when it is the water of truth, and not to disdain cold frogs and hot toads?

Or is it this: to love those who despise us and to offer our hand to the ghost when it wants to frighten us?

The weight-bearing spirit takes upon itself all these heaviest things: like a camel hurrying laden into the desert, thus it hurries into its desert.

But in the loneliest desert the second metamorphosis occurs: the spirit here becomes a lion; it wants to capture freedom and be lord in its own desert.

It seeks here its ultimate lord: it will be an enemy to him and to its ultimate God, it will struggle for victory with the great dragon.

What is the great dragon which the spirit no longer wants to call lord and God? The great dragon is called 'Thou shalt'. But the spirit of the lion says 'I will!'

'Thou shalt' lies in its path, sparkling with gold, a scale-covered breast, and on every scale glitters golden 'Thou shalt'.

Values of a thousand years glitter on the scales, and thus speaks the mightiest of all dragons: 'All the values of things – glitter on me.

'All values have already been created, and all created values – are in me. Truly, there shall be no more "I will"!' Thus speaks the dragon.

My brothers, why is the lion needed in the spirit? Why does the beast of burden, that renounces and is reverent, not suffice?

To create new values – even the lion is capable of that: but to create itself freedom for new creation – that the might of the lion can do.

To create freedom for itself and a sacred No even to duty: the lion is needed for that, my brothers.

To seize the right to new values – that is the most terrible proceeding for a weight-bearing and reverential spirit. Truly, to this spirit it is a theft and a work for an animal of prey.

Once it loved this 'Thou shalt' as its holiest thing: now it has to find illusion and caprice even in the holiest, that it may steal freedom from its love: the lion is needed for this theft.

But tell me, my brothers, what can the child do that even the lion cannot? Why must the preying lion still become a child?

The child is innocence and forgetfulness, a new beginning, a sport, a self-propelling wheel, a first motion, a sacred Yes.

Yes, a sacred Yes is needed, my brothers, for the sport of creation: the spirit now wills *its own* will, the spirit sundered from the world now wins *its own* world.

I have named you three metamorphoses of the spirit: how the spirit became a camel, and the camel a lion, and the lion at last a child.

Thus spoke Zarathustra. And at that time he was living in the town called The Pied Cow.

OF THE CHAIRS OF VIRTUE

ZARATHUSTRA heard a wise man praised who was said to discourse well on sleep and virtue: he was greatly honoured and rewarded for it, and all the young men sat before his chair. Zarathustra went to him and sat before his chair with all the young men. And thus spoke the wise man:

•

Honour to sleep and modesty before it! That is the first thing! And avoid all those who sleep badly and are awake at night!

Even the thief is shamed when confronted with sleep: he always steals softly through the night. But shameless is the night-watchman, shamelessly he bears his horn.

Sleeping is no mean art: you need to stay awake all day to do it.

You must overcome yourself ten times a day: that causes a fine weariness and is opium to the soul.

Ten times must you be reconciled to yourself again: for overcoming is bitterness and the unreconciled man sleeps badly.

You must discover ten truths a day: otherwise you will seek truth in the night too, with your soul still hungry.

You must laugh and be cheerful ten times a day: or your stomach, that father of affliction, will disturb you in the night.

Few know it, but one must have all the virtues in order to sleep well. Shall I bear false witness? Shall I commit adultery?

Shall I covet my neighbour's maidservant? None of this would be consistent with good sleep.

And even when one has all the virtues, there is still one thing to remember: to send even these virtues to sleep at the proper time.

That they may not quarrel among themselves, the pretty little women! And over you, unhappy man!

Peace with God and with your neighbour: thus good sleep will have it. And peace too with your neighbour's devil. Otherwise he will haunt you at night.

Honour and obedience to the authorities, and even to the crooked authorities! Thus good sleep will have it. How can I help it that power likes to walk on crooked legs?

I shall always carry him the best herdsman who leads his sheep to the greenest meadows: that accords with good sleep.

I do not desire much honour, nor great treasure: they excite spleen. But one sleeps badly without a good name and a small treasure.

The company of a few is more welcome to me than bad company: but they must come and go at the proper time. That accords with good sleep.

The poor in spirit, too, please me greatly: they further sleep. Blessed and happy they are needed, especially if one always agrees with their views.

Thus for the virtuous man does the day pass. And when night comes I take good care not to summon sleep! He, the lord of virtues, does not like to be summoned!

But I remember what I have done and thought during the day. Ruminating I ask myself, patient as a cow: What were your ten overcomings?

And which were the ten reconciliations and the ten truths and the ten fits of laughter with which my heart enjoyed itself?

As I ponder such things rocked by my forty thoughts, sleep, the lord of virtue, suddenly overtakes me uncalled.

Sleep knocks on my eyes: they grow heavy. Sleep touches my mouth: it stays open.

Truly, he comes to me on soft soles, the dearest of thieves, and steals my thoughts from me: I stand as silent as this chair.

But I do not stand for long: already I am lying down.

When Zarathustra heard the wise man's words he laughed in his heart: for through them a light had dawned upon him. And he spoke thus to his heart:

This wise man with his forty thoughts seems to me a fool: but I believe he knows well enough how to sleep.

Happy is he who lives in this wise man's neighbourhood. Such sleep is contagious, even through a thick wall.

A spell dwells even in his chair. And the young men have not sat in vain before the preacher of virtue.

His wisdom is: stay awake in order to sleep well. And truly, if life had no sense and I had to choose nonsense, this would be the most desirable nonsense for me, too.

Now it is clear to me what people were once seeking above all when they sought the teachers of virtue. They sought good sleep and opium virtues to bring it about!

To all of these lauded wise men of the academic chairs, wisdom meant sleep without dreams: they knew no better meaning of life.

And today too there are some like this preacher of virtue, and not always so honourable: but their time is up. And they shall not stand for much longer: already they are lying down.

Blessed are these drowsy men: for they shall soon drop off.

Thus spoke Zarathustra.

ONCE Zarathustra too cast his deluded fancy beyond mankind, like all afterworldsmen. Then the world seemed to me the work of a suffering and tormented God.

Then the world seemed to me the dream and fiction of a God; coloured vapour before the eyes of a discontented God.

Good and evil and joy and sorrow and I and You – I thought them coloured vapour before the creator's eyes. The creator wanted to look away from himself, so he created the world.

It is intoxicating joy for the sufferer to look away from his suffering and to forget himself. Intoxicating joy and self-forgetting – that is what I once thought the world.

This world, the eternally imperfect, the eternal and imperfect image of a contradiction – an intoxicating joy to its imperfect creator – that is what I once thought the world.

Thus I too once cast my deluded fancy beyond mankind, like all afterworldsmen. Beyond mankind in reality?

Ah, brothers, this God which I created was human work and human madness, like all gods!

He was human, and a poor piece of man and Ego: this phantom came to me from my own fire and ashes, that is the truth! It did not come to me from the 'beyond'!

What happened, my brothers? I, the sufferer, overcame myself, I carried my own ashes to the mountains, I made for myself a brighter flame. And behold! the phantom *fled* from me!

Now to me, the convalescent, it would be suffering and torment to believe in such phantoms: it would be suffering to me now and humiliation. Thus I speak to the afterworldsmen.

It was suffering and impotence – that created all afterworlds; and that brief madness of happiness that only the greatest sufferer experiences.

Weariness, which wants to reach the ultimate with a single leap, with a death-leap, a poor ignorant weariness, which no longer wants even to want: that created all gods and afterworlds.

Believe me, my brothers! It was the body that despaired of the body – that touched the ultimate walls with the fingers of its deluded spirit.

Believe me, my brothers! It was the body that despaired of the earth – that heard the belly of being speak to it.

And then it wanted to get its head through the ultimate walls – and not its head only – over into the 'other world'.

But that 'other world', that inhuman, dehumanized world which is a heavenly Nothing, is well hidden from men; and the belly of being does not speak to man, except as man.

Truly, all being is hard to demonstrate; it is hard to make it speak. Yet, tell me, brothers, is not the most wonderful of all things most clearly demonstrated?

Yes, this Ego, with its contradiction and confusion, speaks most honestly of its being – this creating, willing, evaluating Ego, which is the measure and value of things.

And this most honest being, the Ego – it speaks of the body, and it insists upon the body, even when it fables and fabricates and flutters with broken wings.

Ever more honestly it learns to speak, the Ego: and the more it learns, the more it finds titles and honours for the body and the earth.

My Ego taught me a new pride, I teach it to men: No longer to bury the head in the sand of heavenly things, but to carry it freely, an earthly head which creates meaning for the earth!

I teach mankind a new will: to desire this path that men have followed blindly, and to call it good and no more to creep aside from it, like the sick and dying!

It was the sick and dying who despised the body and the earth and invented the things of heaven and the redeeming drops of blood: but even these sweet and dismal poisons they took from the body and the earth!

They wanted to escape from their misery and the stars were too far for them. Then they sighed: 'Oh if only there were heavenly paths by which to creep into another existence and into happiness!' – then they contrived for themselves their secret ways and their draughts of blood!

Now they thought themselves transported from their bodies and from this earth, these ingrates. Yet to what do they owe the convulsion and joy of their transport? To their bodies and to this earth.

Zarathustra is gentle with the sick. Truly, he is not angry at their manner of consolation and ingratitude. May they become convalescents and overcomers and make for themselves a higher body!

Neither is Zarathustra angry with the convalescent if he glances tenderly at his illusions and creeps at midnight around the grave of his God; but even his tears still speak to me of sickness and a sick body.

There have always been many sickly people among those who invent fables and long for God: they have a raging hate for the enlightened man and for that youngest of virtues which is called honesty.

They are always looking back to dark ages: then, indeed, illusion and faith were a different question; raving of the reason was likeness to God, and doubt was sin.

I know these Godlike people all too well: they want to be believed in, and doubt to be sin. I also know all too well what it is they themselves most firmly believe in.

Truly not in afterworlds and redeeming drops of blood: they believe most firmly in the body, and their own body is for them their thing-in-itself.

But it is a sickly thing to them: and they would dearly like to get out of their skins. That is why they hearken to preachers of death and themselves preach afterworlds.

Listen rather, my brothers, to the voice of the healthy body: this is a purer voice and a more honest one.

Purer and more honest of speech is the healthy body, perfect and square-built: and it speaks of the meaning of the earth.

Thus spoke Zarathustra.

I WISH to speak to the despisers of the body. Let them not learn differently nor teach differently, but only bid farewell to their own bodies – and so become dumb.

'I am body and soul' – so speaks the child. And why should one not speak like children?

But the awakened, the enlightened man says: I am body entirely, and nothing beside; and soul is only a word for something in the body.

The body is a great intelligence, a multiplicity with one sense, a war and a peace, a herd and a herdsman.

Your little intelligence, my brother, which you call 'spirit', is also an instrument of your body, a little instrument and toy of your great intelligence.

You say 'I' and you are proud of this word. But greater than this – although you will not believe in it – is your body and its great intelligence, which does not say 'I' but performs 'I'.

What the sense feels, what the spirit perceives, is never an end in itself. But sense and spirit would like to persuade you that they are the end of all things: they are as vain as that.

Sense and spirit are instruments and toys: behind them still lies the Self. The Self seeks with the eyes of the sense, it listens too with the ears of the spirit.

The Self is always listening and seeking: it compares,

subdues, conquers, destroys. It rules and is also the Ego's ruler.

Behind your thoughts and feelings, my brother, stands a mighty commander, an unknown sage – he is called Self. He lives in your body, he is your body.

There is more reason in your body than in your best wisdom. And who knows for what purpose your body requires precisely your best wisdom?

Your Self laughs at your Ego and its proud leapings. 'What are these leapings and flights of thought to me?' it says to itself. 'A by-way to my goal. I am the Ego's leading-string and I prompt its conceptions.'

The Self says to the Ego: 'Feel pain!' Thereupon it suffers and gives thought how to end its suffering – and it is *meant* to think for just that purpose.

The Self says to the Ego: 'Feel joy!' Thereupon it rejoices and gives thought how it may often rejoice – and it is *meant* to think for just that purpose.

I want to say a word to the despisers of the body. It is their esteem that produces this disesteem. What is it that created esteem and disesteem and value and will?

The creative Self created for itself esteem and disesteem, it created for itself joy and sorrow. The creative body created spirit for itself, as a hand of its will.

Even in your folly and contempt, you despisers of the body, you serve your Self. I tell you: your Self itself wants to die and turn away from life.

Your Self can no longer perform that act which it most desires to perform: to create beyond itself. That is what it most wishes to do, that is its whole ardour.

But now it has grown too late for that: so your Self wants to perish, you despisers of the body.

Your Self wants to perish, and that is why you have become despisers of the body! For no longer are you able to create beyond yourselves.

And therefore you are now angry with life and with the earth. An unconscious envy lies in the sidelong glance of your contempt.

I do not go your way, you despisers of the body! You are not bridges to the Superman!

Thus spoke Zarathustra.

OF JOYS AND PASSIONS

MY brother, if you have virtue and it is your own virtue, you have it in common with no one.

To be sure, you want to call it by a name and caress it; you want to pull its ears and amuse yourself with it.

And behold! Now you have its name in common with the people and have become of the people and the herd with your virtue!

You would do better to say: 'Unutterable and nameless is that which torments and delights the soul and is also the hunger of my belly.'

Let your virtue be too exalted for the familiarity of names: and if you have to speak of it, do not be ashamed to stammer.

Thus say and stammer: 'This is *my* good, this I love, just thus do I like it, only thus do *I* wish the good.

'I do not want it as a law of God, I do not want it as a human statute: let it be no sign-post to superearths and paradises.

'It is an earthly virtue that I love: there is little prudence in it, and least of all common wisdom.

'But this bird has built its nest beneath my roof: therefore I love and cherish it – now it sits there upon its golden eggs.'

Thus should you stammer and praise your virtue.

Once you had passions and called them evil. But now you have only your virtues: they grew from out your passions.

You laid your highest aim in the heart of these passions: then they became your virtues and joys.

And though you came from the race of the hot-tempered or of the lustful or of the fanatical or of the vindictive:

At last all your passions have become virtues and all your devils angels.

Once you had fierce dogs in your cellar: but they changed at last into birds and sweet singers.

From your poison you brewed your balsam; you milked your cow, affliction, now you drink the sweet milk of her udder.

And henceforward nothing evil shall come out of you, except it be the evil that comes from the conflict of your virtues.

My brother, if you are lucky you will have one virtue and no more: thus you will go more easily over the bridge.

To have many virtues is to be distinguished, but it is a hard fate; and many a man has gone into the desert and killed himself because he was tired of being a battle and battle-ground of virtues.

My brother, are war and battle evil? But this evil is necessary, envy and mistrust and calumny among your virtues is necessary.

Behold how each of your virtues desires the highest place: it wants your entire spirit, that your spirit may be *its* herald, it wants your entire strength in anger, hate and love.

Every virtue is jealous of the others, and jealousy is a terrible thing. Even virtues can be destroyed through jealousy.

He whom the flames of jealousy surround at last turns his poisoned sting against himself, like the scorpion.

Ah my brother, have you never yet seen a virtue turn upon itself and stab itself.

Man is something that must be overcome: and for that reason you must love your virtues – for you will perish by them.

Thus spoke Zarathustra.

OF THE PALE CRIMINAL

You do not intend to kill, you judges and sacrificers, before the beast has bowed its neck? Behold, the pale criminal has bowed his neck: from his eye speaks the great contempt.

'My Ego is something that should be overcome: my Ego is to me the great contempt of man': that is what this eye says.

He judged himself – that was his supreme moment: do not let the exalted man relapse again into his lowly condition!

There is no redemption for him who thus suffers from himself, except it be a quick death.

Your killing, you judges, should be a mercy and not a revenge. And since you kill, see to it that you yourselves justify life!

It is not sufficient that you should be reconciled with him you kill. May your sorrow be love for the Superman: thus will you justify your continuing to live!

You should say 'enemy', but not 'miscreant'; you should say 'invalid', but not 'scoundrel'; you should say 'fool', but not 'sinner'.

And you, scarlet judge, if you would speak aloud all you have done in thought, everyone would cry: 'Away with this filth and poisonous snake!'

But the thought is one thing, the deed is another, and another yet is the image of the deed. The wheel of causality does not roll between them.

An image made this pale man pale. He was equal to his deed when he did it: but he could not endure its image after it was done.

Now for evermore he saw himself as the perpetrator of one deed. I call this madness: in him the exception has become the rule.

The chalk-line charmed the hen; the blow he struck charmed his simple mind – I call this madness *after* the deed.

Listen, you judges! There is another madness as well; and it comes *before* the deed. Ah, you have not crept deep enough into this soul!

Thus says the scarlet judge: 'Why did this criminal murder? He wanted to steal.' But I tell you: his soul wanted blood not booty: he thirsted for the joy of the knife!

But his simple mind did not understand this madness and it persuaded him otherwise. 'What is the good of blood?' it said. 'Will you not at least commit a theft too? Take a revenge?'

And he hearkened to his simple mind: its words lay like lead upon him – then he robbed as he murdered. He did not want to be ashamed of his madness.

And now again the lead of his guilt lies upon him, and again his simple mind is so numb, so paralysed, so heavy.

If only he could shake his head his burden would roll off: but who can shake his head?

What is this man? A heap of diseases that reach out into the world through the spirit: there they want to catch their prey.

What is this man? A knot of savage serpents that are seldom at peace among themselves – thus they go forth alone to seek prey in the world.

Behold this poor body! This poor soul interpreted to itself what this body suffered and desired – it interpreted it as lust for murder and greed for the joy of the knife.

The evil which is now evil overtakes him who now becomes sick: he wants to do harm with that which harms him. But there have been other ages and another evil and good.

Once doubt and the will to Self were evil. Then the invalid became heretic and witch: as heretic and witch he suffered and wanted to cause suffering.

But this will not enter your ears: you tell me it hurts your good people. But what are your good people to me?

Much about your good people moves me to disgust, and it is not their evil I mean. How I wish they possessed a madness through which they could perish, like this pale criminal.

Truly, I wish their madness were called truth or loyalty or justice: but they possess their virtue in order to live long and in a miserable ease.

I am a railing beside the stream: he who can grasp me, let him grasp me! I am not, however, your crutch.

Thus spoke Zarathustra.

OF READING AND WRITING

Of all writings I love only that which is written with blood. Write with blood: and you will discover that blood is spirit.

It is not an easy thing to understand unfamiliar blood: I hate the reading idler.

He who knows the reader, does nothing further for the reader. Another century of readers – and spirit itself will stink.

That everyone can learn to read will ruin in the long run not only writing, but thinking too.

Once spirit was God, then it became man, and now it is even becoming mob.

He who writes in blood and aphorisms does not want to be read, he wants to be learned by heart.

In the mountains the shortest route is from peak to peak, but for that you must have long legs. Aphorisms should be peaks, and those to whom they are spoken should be big and tall of stature.

The air thin and pure, danger near, and the spirit full of a joyful wickedness: these things suit one another.

I want hobgoblins around me, for I am courageous. Courage that scares away phantoms makes hobgoblins for itself – courage wants to laugh.

I no longer feel as you do: this cloud which I see under me, this blackness and heaviness at which I laugh – precisely this is your thunder-cloud.

You look up when you desire to be exalted. And I look down, because I am exalted.

Who among you can at the same time laugh and be exalted?

He who climbs upon the highest mountains laughs at all tragedies, real or imaginary.

Untroubled, scornful, outrageous – that is how wisdom wants us to be: she is a woman and never loves anyone but a warrior.

You tell me: 'Life is hard to bear.' But if it were otherwise why should you have your pride in the morning and your resignation in the evening?

Life is hard to bear: but do not pretend to be so tender! We are all of us pretty fine asses and assesses of burden!

What have we in common with the rosebud, which trembles because a drop of dew is lying upon it?

It is true: we love life, not because we are used to living but because we are used to loving.

There is always a certain madness in love. But also there is always a certain method in madness.

And to me too, who love life, it seems that butterflies and soap-bubbles, and whatever is like them among men, know most about happiness.

To see these light, foolish, dainty, affecting little souls flutter about – that moves Zarathustra to tears and to song.

I should believe only in a God who understood how to dance.

And when I beheld my devil, I found him serious, thorough, profound, solemn: it was the Spirit of Gravity – through him all things are ruined.

One does not kill by anger but by laughter. Come, let us kill the Spirit of Gravity!

I have learned to walk: since then I have run. I have learned to fly: since then I do not have to be pushed in order to move.

Now I am nimble, now I fly, now I see myself under myself, now a god dances within me.

Thus spoke Zarathustra.

OF THE TREE ON THE MOUNTAINSIDE

ZARATHUSTRA had noticed that a young man was avoiding him. And as he was walking alone one evening through the mountains surrounding the town called The Pied Cow, behold he found this young man leaning against a tree and gazing wearily into the valley. Zarathustra grasped the tree beside which the young man was sitting and spoke thus:

'If I wanted to shake this tree with my hands I should be unable to do it.

'But the wind, which we cannot see, torments it and bends it where it wishes. It is invisible hands that torment and bend us the worst.'

At that the young man stood up in confusion and said: 'I hear Zarathustra and I was just thinking of him.'

Zarathustra replied: 'Why are you alarmed on that account? – Now it is with men as with this tree.

'The more it wants to rise into the heights and the light, the more determinedly do its roots strive earthwards, downwards, into the darkness, into the depths – into evil.'

'Yes, into evil!' cried the young man. 'How is it possible you can uncover my soul?'

Zarathustra smiled and said: 'There are many souls one will never uncover, unless one invents them first.'

'Yes, into evil!' cried the young man again.

'You have spoken the truth, Zarathustra. Since I wanted to rise into the heights I have no longer trusted myself, and no one trusts me any more. How did this happen?

'I change too quickly: my today refutes my yesterday. When I ascend I often jump over steps, and no step forgives me that.

'When I am aloft, I always find myself alone. No one speaks to me, the frost of solitude makes me tremble. What do I want in the heights?

'My contempt and my desire increase together; the higher I

climb, the more do I despise him who climbs. What do I want in the heights?

'How ashamed I am of my climbing and stumbling! How I scorn my violent panting! How I hate the man who can fly! How weary I am in the heights!'

Here the young man fell silent. And Zarathustra contemplated the tree beside which they were standing, and spoke thus:

'This tree stands here alone on the mountainside; it has grown up high above a man and animal.

'And if it wished to speak, it would find no one who understood it: so high has it grown.

'Now it waits and waits – yet what is it waiting for? It lives too near the seat of the clouds: is it waiting, perhaps, for the first lightning?'

When Zarathustra said this, the young man cried with violent gestures: 'Yes, Zarathustra, you speak true. I desired my destruction when I wanted to ascend into the heights, and you are the lightning for which I have been waiting! Behold, what have I been since you appeared among us? It is *envy* of you which has destroyed me!' Thus spoke the young man and wept bitterly. But Zarathustra laid his arm about him and drew him along with him.

And when they had been walking together for a while, Zarathustra began to speak thus:

It breaks my heart. Better than your words, your eye tells me all your peril.

You are not yet free, you still *search* for freedom. Your search has fatigued you and made you too wakeful.

You long for the open heights, your soul thirsts for the stars. But your bad instincts too thirst for freedom.

Your fierce dogs long for freedom; they bark for joy in their cellar when your spirit aspires to break open all prisons.

To me you are still a prisoner who imagines freedom: ah, such prisoners of the soul become clever, but also deceitful and base.

The free man of the spirit, too, must still purify himself. Much of the prison and rottenness still remain within him: his eye still has to become pure.

Yes, I know your peril. But, by my hope and hope I entreat you: do not reject your love and hope!

You still feel yourself noble, and the others, too, who dislike you and cast evil glances at you, still feel you are noble. Learn that everyone finds the noble man an obstruction.

The good, too, find the noble man an obstruction: and even when they call him a good man they do so in order to make away with him.

The noble man wants to create new things and a new virtue. The good man wants the old things and that the old things shall be preserved.

But that is not the danger for the noble man – that he may become a good man – but that he may become an impudent one, a derider, a destroyer.

Alas, I have known noble men who lost their highest hope. And henceforth they slandered all high hopes.

Henceforth they lived impudently in brief pleasures, and they had hardly an aim beyond the day.

'Spirit is also sensual pleasure' – thus they spoke. Then the wings of their spirit broke: now it creeps around and it makes dirty what it feeds on.

Once they thought of becoming heroes: now they are sensualists. The hero is to them an affliction and a terror.

But, by my love and hope I entreat you: do not reject the hero in your soul! Keep holy your highest hope!

Thus spoke Zarathustra.

OF THE PREACHERS OF DEATH

THERE are preachers of death: and the earth is full of those to whom departure from life must be preached.

The earth is full of the superfluous, life has been corrupted by the many-too-many. Let them be lured by 'eternal life' out of this life!

Yellow men or black men: that is what the preachers of death are called. But I want to show them to you in other colours.

There are the dreadful creatures who carry a beast of prey round with them, and have no choice except lusts or self-mortification. And even their lusts are self-mortification.

They have not yet even become men, these dreadful creatures. Let them preach departure from life and depart themselves!

There are the consumptives of the soul: they are hardly born before they begin to die and to long for doctrines of weariness and renunciation.

They would like to be dead, and we should approve their

wish! Let us guard against awakening these dead men and damaging these living coffins.

They encounter an invalid or an old man or a corpse; and straightaway they say 'Life is refuted!'

But only they are refuted, they and their eye that sees only one aspect of existence.

Muffled in deep depression, and longing for the little accidents that bring about death: thus they wait and clench their teeth.

Or: they snatch at sweets and in doing so mock their childishness: they cling to their straw of life and mock that they are still clinging to a straw.

Their wisdom runs: 'He who goes on living is a fool, but we are such fools! And precisely that is the most foolish thing in life!'

'Life is only suffering' – thus others of them speak, and they do not lie: so see to it that *you* cease to live! So see to it that the life which is only suffering ceases!

And let the teaching of your virtue be: 'You shall kill yourself! You shall steal away from yourself!'

'Lust is sin' – thus say some who preach death – 'let us go aside and beget no children!'

'Giving birth is laborious' – say others – 'why go on giving birth? One gives birth only to unhappy children!' And they too are preachers of death.

'Men are to be pitied' – thus say others again. 'Take what I have! Take what I am! By so much less am I bound to life!'

If they were compassionate from the very heart they would seek to make their neighbours disgusted with life. To be evil – that would be their true good.

But they want to escape from life: what is it to them that, with their chains and gifts, they bind others still more firmly to it?

And you too, you to whom life is unrestrained labour and anxiety: are you not very weary of life? Are you not very ripe for the sermon of death?

All of you, to whom unrestrained labour, and the swift, the new, the strange, are dear, you endure yourselves ill, your industry is flight and will to forget yourselves.

If you believed more in life, you would devote yourselves less to the moment. But you have insufficient capacity for waiting – or even for laziness!

Everywhere resound the voices of those who preach death: and the earth is full of those to whom death must be preached.

Or 'eternal life': it is all the same to me – provided they pass away quickly!

Thus spoke Zarathustra.

OF WAR AND WARRIORS

WE do not wish to be spared by our best enemies, nor by those whom we love from the very heart. So let me tell you the truth!

My brother in war! I love you from the very heart, I am and have always been of your kind. And I am also your best enemy. So let me tell you the truth!

I know the hatred and envy of your hearts. You are not

great enough not to know hatred and envy. So be great enough not to be ashamed of them!

And if you cannot be saints of knowledge, at least be its warriors. They are the companions and forerunners of such sainthood.

I see many soldiers: if only I could see many warriors! What they wear is called uniform: may what they conceal with it not be uniform too!

You should be such men as are always looking for an enemy – for *your* enemy. And with some of you there is hate at first sight.

You should seek your enemy, you should wage your war – a war for your opinions. And if your opinion is defeated, your honesty should still cry triumph over that!

You should love peace as a means to new wars. And the short peace more than the long.

I do not exhort you to work but to battle. I do not exhort you to peace, but to victory. May your work be battle, may your peace be victory!

One can be silent and sit still only when one has arrow and bow: otherwise one babbles and quarrels. May your peace be a victory!

You say it is the good cause that hallows even war? I tell you: it is the good war that hallows every cause.

War and courage have done more great things than charity. Not your pity but your bravery has saved the unfortunate up to now.

'What is good?' you ask. To be brave is good. Let the little girls say: 'To be good is to be what is pretty and at the same time touching.'

They call you heartless: but your heart is true, and I love the modesty of your kind-heartedness. You feel ashamed of your flow, while others feel ashamed of their ebb.

Are you ugly? Very well, my brothers! Take the sublime about you, the mantle of the ugly!

And when your soul grows great, it grows arrogant, and there is wickedness in your sublimity. I know you.

In wickedness, the arrogant and the weak man meet. But they misunderstand one another. I know you.

You may have enemies whom you hate, but not enemies whom you despise. You must be proud of your enemy: then the success of your enemy shall be your success too.

To rebel – that shows nobility in a slave. Let your nobility show itself in obeying! Let even your commanding be an obeying!

To a good warrior, 'thou shalt' sounds more agreeable than 'I will'. And everything that is dear to you, you should first have commanded to you.

Let your love towards life be love towards your highest hope: and let your highest hope be the highest idea of life!

But you should let me commend to you your highest idea – and it is: Man is something that should be overcome.

Thus live your life of obedience and war! What good is long life? What warrior wants to be spared?

I do not spare you, I love you from the very heart, my brothers in war!

Thus spoke Zarathustra.

THERE are still peoples and herds somewhere, but not with us, my brothers: here there are states.

The state? What is that? Well then! Now open your ears, for now I shall speak to you of the death of peoples.

The state is the coldest of all cold monsters. Coldly it lies, too: and this lie creeps from its mouth: 'I, the state, am the people.'

It is a lie! It was creators who created peoples and hung a faith and a love over them: thus they served life.

It is destroyers who set snares for many and call it the state: they hang a sword and a hundred desires over them.

Where a people still exists, there the people do not understand the state and hate it as the evil eye and sin against custom and law.

I offer you this sign: every people speaks its own language of good and evil: its neighbour does not understand this language. It invented this language for itself in custom and law.

But the state lies in all languages of good and evil; and whatever it says, it lies – and whatever it has, it has stolen.

Everything about it is false; it bites with stolen teeth. Even its belly is false.

Confusion of the language of good and evil; I offer you this sign as the sign of the state. Truly, this sign indicates the will to death! Truly, it beckons to the preachers of death!

Many too many are born: the state was invented for the superfluous!

Just see how it lures them, the many-to-many! How it devours them, and chews them, and re-chews them!

'There is nothing greater on earth than I, the regulating finger of God' – thus the monster bellows. And not only the long-eared and short-sighted sink to their knees!

Ah, it whispers its dismal lies to you too, you great souls! Ah, it divines the abundant hearts that like to squander themselves!

Yes, it divines you too, you conquerors of the old God! You grew weary in battle and now your weariness serves the new idol!

It would like to range heroes and honourable men about it, this new idol! It likes to sun itself in the sunshine of good consciences – this cold monster!

It will give *you* everything if *you* worship it, this new idol: thus it buys for itself the lustre of your virtues and the glance of your proud eyes.

It wants to use you to lure the many-too-many. Yes, a cunning device of Hell has here been devised, a horse of death jingling with the trappings of divine honours!

Yes, a death for many has here been devised that glorifies itself as life: truly, a heart-felt service to all preachers of death!

I call it the state where everyone, good and bad, is a poison-drinker: the state where everyone, good and bad, loses himself: the state where universal slow suicide is called – life.

Just look at these superfluous people! They steal for themselves the works of inventors and the treasures of the wise: they call their theft culture – and they turn everything to sickness and calamity.

Just look at these superfluous people! They are always ill, they vomit their bile and call it a newspaper. They devour one another and cannot even digest themselves.

Just look at these superfluous people! They acquire wealth and make themselves poorer with it. They desire power and especially the lever of power, plenty of money – these impotent people!

See them clamber, these nimble apes! They clamber over one another and so scuffle into the mud and the abyss.

They all strive towards the throne: it is a madness they have – as if happiness sat upon the throne! Often filth sits upon the throne – and often the throne upon filth, too.

They all seem madmen to me and clambering apes and too vehement. Their idol, that cold monster, smells unpleasant to me: all of them, all these idolators, smell unpleasant to me.

My brothers, do you then want to suffocate in the fumes of their animal mouths and appetites? Better to break the window and leap into the open air.

Avoid this bad odour! Leave the idolatry of the superfluous!

Avoid this bad odour! Leave the smoke of these human sacrifices!

The earth still remains free for great souls. Many places – the odour of tranquil seas blowing about them – are still empty for solitaries and solitary couples.

A free life still remains for great souls. Truly, he who possesses little is so much the less possessed: praised be a moderate poverty!

Only there, where the state ceases, does the man who is not

superfluous begin: does the song of the necessary man, the unique and irreplaceable melody begin.

There, where the state *ceases* – look there, my brothers. Do you not see it: the rainbow and the bridges to the Superman?

Thus spoke Zarathustra.

OF THE FLIES OF THE MARKET-PLACE

FLEE, my friend, into your solitude! I see you deafened by the uproar of the great men and pricked by the stings of the small ones.

Forest and rock know well how to be silent with you. Be like the tree again, the wide-branching tree that you love: calmly and attentively it leans out over the sea.

Where solitude ceases, there the market-place begins; and where the market-place begins, there begins the uproar of the great actors and the buzzing of the poisonous flies.

In the world even the best things are worthless apart from him who first presents them: people call these presenters 'great men'.

The people have little idea of greatness, that is to say: creativeness. But they have a taste for all presenters and actors of great things.

The world revolves about the inventor of new values: imperceptibly it revolves. But the people and the glory revolve around the actor: that is 'the way of the world'.

The actor possesses spirit but little conscience of the spirit.

He always believes in that with which he most powerfully produces belief – produces belief in *himself*!

Tomorrow he will have a new faith and the day after tomorrow a newer one. He has a quick perception, as the people have, and a capricious temperament.

To overthrow – to him that means: to prove. To drive frantic – to him that means: to convince. And blood is to him the best of all arguments.

A truth that penetrates only sensitive ears he calls a lie and a thing of nothing. Truly, he believes only in gods who make a great noise in the world!

The market-place is full of solemn buffoons – and the people boast of their great men! These are their heroes of the hour.

But the hour presses them: so they press you. And from you too they require a Yes or a No. And woe to you if you want to set your chair between For and Against.

Do not be jealous, lover of truth, because of these inflexible and oppressive men! Truth has never yet clung to the arm of an inflexible man.

Return to your security because of these abrupt men: only in the market-place is one assailed with Yes? or No?

The experience of all deep wells is slow: they must wait long until they know *what* has fallen into their depths.

All great things occur away from glory and the market-place: the inventors of new values have always lived away from glory and the market-place.

Flee, my friend, into your solitude: I see you stung by poisonous flies. Flee to where the raw, rough breeze blows!

Flee into your solitude! You have lived too near the small and the pitiable men. Flee from their hidden vengeance! Towards you they are nothing but vengeance.

No longer lift your arm against them! They are innumerable and it is not your fate to be a fly-swat.

Innumerable are these small and pitiable men; and raindrops and weeds have already brought about the destruction of many a proud building.

You are no stone, but already these many drops have made you hollow. You will yet break and burst apart through these many drops.

I see you wearied by poisonous flies, I see you bloodily torn in a hundred places; and your pride refuses even to be angry.

They want blood from you in all innocence, their bloodless souls thirst for blood – and therefore they sting in all innocence.

But you, profound man, you suffer too profoundly even from small wounds; and before you have recovered, the same poison-worm is again crawling over your hand.

You are too proud to kill these sweet-toothed creatures. But take care that it does not become your fate to bear all their poisonous injustice!

They buzz around you even with their praise: and their praise is importunity. They want to be near your skin and your blood.

They flatter you as if you were a god or a devil; they whine before you as before a god or a devil. What of it! They are flatterers and whiners, and nothing more.

And they are often kind to you. But that has always been the prudence of the cowardly. Yes, the cowardly are prudent!

They think about you a great deal with their narrow souls – you are always suspicious to them. Everything that is thought about a great deal is finally thought suspicious.

They punish you for all your virtues. Fundamentally they forgive you only – your mistakes.

Because you are gentle and just-minded, you say: 'They are not to be blamed for their little existence.' But their little souls think: 'All great existence is blameworthy.'

Even when you are gentle towards them, they still feel you despise them: and they return your kindness with secret unkindness.

Your silent pride always offends their taste; they rejoice if you are ever modest enough to be vain.

When we recognize a peculiarity in a man we also inflame that peculiarity. So guard yourself against the small men!

Before you, they feel themselves small, and their baseness glimmers and glows against you in hidden vengeance.

Have you not noticed how often they became silent when you approached them, and how their strength left them like smoke from a dying fire?

Yes, my friend, you are a bad conscience to your neighbours: for they are unworthy of you. Thus they hate you and would dearly like to suck your blood.

Your neighbours will always be poisonous flies: that about you which is great, that itself must make them more poisonous and ever more fly-like.

Flee, my friend, into your solitude and to where the raw, rough breeze blows! It is not your fate to be a fly-swat.

Thus spoke Zarathustra.

OF CHASTITY

I LOVE the forest. It is bad to live in towns: too many of the lustful live there.

Is it not better to fall into the hands of a murderer than into the dreams of a lustful woman?

And just look at these men: their eye reveals it – they know of nothing better on earth than to lie with a woman.

There is filth at the bottom of their souls; and it is worse if this filth has something of the spirit in it!

If only you had become perfect at least as animals! But to animals belongs innocence.

Do I exhort you to kill your senses? I exhort you to an innocence of the senses.

Do I exhort you to chastity? With some, chastity is a virtue, but with many it is almost a vice.

These people abstain, it is true: but the bitch Sensuality glares enviously out of all they do.

This restless beast follows them even into the heights of their virtue and the depths of their cold spirit.

And how nicely the bitch Sensuality knows how to beg for a piece of spirit, when a piece of flesh is denied her.

Do you love tragedies and all that is heartbreaking? But

mistrust your bitch Sensuality.

Your eyes are too cruel for me; you look upon sufferers lustfully. Has your lasciviousness not merely disguised itself and called itself pity?

And I offer you this parable: Not a few who sought to drive out their devil entered into the swine themselves.

Those to whom chastity is difficult should be dissuaded from it, lest it become the way to Hell – that is, to filth and lust of the soul.

Am I speaking of dirty things? That does not seem to me the worst I could do.

Not when truth is dirty, but when it is shallow, does the enlightened man dislike to wade into its waters.

Truly, there are those who are chaste from the very heart: they are more gentle of heart and they laugh more often and more heartily than you.

They laugh at chastity too, and ask: 'What is chastity?

'Is chastity not folly? But this folly came to us and not we to it.

'We offered this guest love and shelter: now it lives with us – let it stay as long as it wishes!'

Thus spoke Zarathustra.

OF THE FRIEND

'ONE is always one too many around me' – thus speaks the hermit. 'Always once one – in the long run that makes two!'

I and Me are always too earnestly in conversation with one another: how could it be endured, if there were not a friend?

For the hermit the friend is always the third person: the third person is the cork that prevents the conversation of the other two from sinking to the depths.

Alas, for all hermits there are too many depths. That is why they long so much for a friend and for his heights.

Our faith in others betrays wherein we would dearly like to have faith in ourselves. Our longing for a friend is our betrayer.

And often with our love we only want to leap over envy. And often we attack and make an enemy in order to conceal that we are vulnerable to attack.

'At least be my enemy!' – thus speaks the true reverence, that does not venture to ask for friendship.

If you want a friend, you must also be willing to wage war for him: and to wage war, you must be *capable* of being an enemy.

You should honour even the enemy in your friend. Can you go near to your friend without going over to him?

In your friend you should possess your best enemy. Your heart should feel closest to him when you oppose him.

Do you wish to go naked before your friend? Is it in honour of your friend that you show yourself to him as you are? But he wishes you to the Devil for it!

He who makes no secret of himself excites anger in others: that is how much reason you have to fear nakedness! If you were gods you could then be ashamed of your clothes!

You cannot adorn yourself too well for your friend: for you should be to him an arrow and a longing for the Superman.

Have you ever watched your friend asleep – to discover what he looked like? Yet your friend's face is something else beside. It is your own face, in a rough and imperfect mirror.

Have you ever watched your friend asleep? Were you not startled to see what he looked like? O my friend, man is something that must be overcome.

The friend should be a master in conjecture and in keeping silence: you must not want to see everything. Your dream should tell you what your friend does when awake.

May your pity be a conjecture: that you may first know if your friend wants pity. Perhaps what he loves in you is the undimmed eye and the glance of eternity.

Let your pity for your friend conceal itself under a hard shell; you should break a tooth biting upon it. Thus it will have delicacy and sweetness.

Are you pure air and solitude and bread and medicine to your friend? Many a one cannot deliver himself from his own chains and yet he is his friend's deliverer.

Are you a slave? If so, you cannot be a friend. Are you a tyrant? If so, you cannot have friends.

In woman, a slave and a tyrant have all too long been concealed. For that reason, woman is not yet capable of friendship: she knows only love.

In a woman's love is injustice and blindness towards all that she does not love. And in the enlightened love of a woman, too, there is still the unexpected attack and lightning and night, along with the light.

Woman is not yet capable of friendship: women are still cats and birds. Or, at best, cows.

Woman is not yet capable of friendship. But tell me, you men, which of you is yet capable of friendship?

Oh your poverty, you men, and your avarice of soul! As much as you give to your friend I will give even to my enemy, and will not have grown poorer in doing so.

There is comradeship: may there be friendship!

Thus spoke Zarathustra.

OF THE THOUSAND AND ONE GOALS

ZARATHUSTRA has seen many lands and many peoples: thus he has discovered the good and evil of many peoples. Zarathustra has found no greater power on earth than good and evil.

No people could live without evaluating; but if it wishes to maintain itself it must not evaluate as its neighbour evaluates.

Much that seemed good to one people seemed shame and disgrace to another: thus I found. I found much that was called evil in one place was in another decked with purple honours.

One neighbour never understood another: his soul was always amazed at his neighbour's madness and wickedness.

A table of values hangs over every people. Behold, it is the table of its overcomings; behold, it is the voice of its will to power.

What it accounts hard it calls praiseworthy; what it accounts indispensable and hard it calls good; and that which relieves the greatest need, the rare, the hardest of all – it glorifies as holy.

Whatever causes it to rule and conquer and glitter, to the dread and envy of its neighbour, that it accounts the sublimest, the paramount, the evaluation and the meaning of all things.

Truly, my brother, if you only knew a people's need and land and sky and neighbour, you could surely divine the law of its overcomings, and why it is upon this ladder that it mounts towards its hope.

'You should always be the first and outrival all others: your jealous soul should love no one, except your friend' – this precept made the soul of a Greek tremble: in following it he followed his path to greatness.

'To speak the truth and to know well how to handle bow and arrow' – this seemed both estimable and hard to that people from whom I got my name – a name which is both estimable and hard to me.

'To honour father and mother and to do their will even from the roots of the soul': another people hung this table of overcoming over itself and became mighty and eternal with it.

'To practise loyalty and for the sake of loyalty to risk honour and blood even in evil and dangerous causes': another people mastered itself with such teaching, and thus mastering itself it became pregnant and heavy with great hopes.

Truly, men have given themselves all their good and evil. Truly, they did not take it, they did not find it, it did not descend to them as a voice from heaven.

Man first implanted values into things to maintain himself –

he created the meaning of things, a human meaning! Therefore he calls himself: 'Man', that is: the evaluator.

Evaluation is creation: hear it, you creative men! Valuating is itself the value and jewel of all valued things.

Only through evaluation is there value: and without evaluation the nut of existence would be hollow. hear it, you creative men!

A change in values – that means a change in the creators of values. He who has to be a creator always has to destroy.

Peoples were the creators at first; only later were individuals creators. Indeed, the individual himself is still the latest creation.

Once the peoples hung a table of values over themselves. The love that wants to rule and the love that wants to obey created together such tables as these.

Joy in the herd is older than joy in the Ego: and as long as the good conscience is called herd, only the bad conscience says: I.

Truly, the cunning, loveless Ego, that seeks its advantage in the advantage of many – that is not the origin of the herd, but the herd's destruction.

It has always been creators and loving men who created good and evil. Fire of love and fire of anger glow in the names of all virtues.

Zarathustra has seen many lands and many peoples: Zarathustra has found no greater power on earth than the work of these loving men: these works are named 'good' and 'evil'.

Truly, the power of this praising and blaming is a monster

Tell me, who will subdue it for me, brothers? Tell me, who will fasten fetters upon the thousand necks of this beast?

Hitherto there have been a thousand goals, for there have been a thousand peoples. Only fetters are still lacking for these thousand necks, the one goal is still lacking.

Yet tell me, my brothers: if a goal for humanity is still lacking, is there not still lacking – humanity itself?

Thus spoke Zarathustra.

OF LOVE OF ONE'S NEIGHBOUR

You crowd together with your neighbours and have beautiful words for it. But I tell you: Your love of your neighbour is your bad love of yourselves.

You flee to your neighbour away from yourselves and would like to make a virtue of it: but I see through your 'selflessness'.

The 'You' is older than the 'I'; the 'You' has been consecrated, but not yet the 'I': so man crowds towards his neighbour.

Do I exhort you to love of your neighbour? I exhort you rather to flight from your neighbour and to love of the most distant!

Higher than love of one's neighbour stands love of the most distant man and of the man of the future; higher still than love of man I account love of causes and of phantoms.

This phantom that runs along behind you, my brother, is

fairer than you; why do you not give it your flesh and bones? But you are afraid and you run to your neighbour.

You cannot endure to be alone with yourselves and do not love yourselves enough: now you want to mislead your neighbour into love and gild yourselves with his mistake.

I wish rather that you could not endure to be with any kind of neighbour or with your neighbour's neighbour; then you would have to create your friend and his overflowing heart out of yourselves.

You invite in a witness when you want to speak well of yourselves; and when you have misled him into thinking well of you, you then think well of yourselves.

It is not only he who speaks contrary to what he knows who lies, but even more he who speaks contrary to what he does not know. And thus speak of yourselves in your dealings with others and deceive your neighbour with yourselves.

Thus speaks the fool: 'Mixing with people ruins the character, especially when one has none.'

One man runs to his neighbour because he is looking for himself, and another because he wants to lose himself. Your bad love of yourselves makes solitude a prison to you.

It is the distant man who pays for your love of your neighbour; and when there are five of you together, a sixth always has to die.

I do not like your festivals, either: I have found too many actors there, and the audience, too, behaved like actors.

I do not teach you the neighbour but the friend. May the friend be to you a festival of the earth and a foretaste of the Superman.

I teach you the friend and his overflowing heart. But you must understand how to be a sponge if you want to be loved by overflowing hearts.

I teach you the friend in whom the world stands complete, a vessel of the good – the creative friend, who always has a complete world to bestow.

And as the world once dispersed for him, so it comes back to him again, as the evolution of good through evil, as the evolution of design from chance.

May the future and the most distant be the principle of your today: in your friend you should love the Superman as your principle.

My brothers, I do not exhort you to love of your neighbour: I exhort you to love of the most distant.

Thus spoke Zarathustra.

OF THE WAY OF THE CREATOR

My brother, do you want to go apart and be alone? Do you want to seek the way to yourself? Pause just a moment and listen to me.

'He who seeks may easily get lost himself. It is a crime to go apart and be alone' – thus speaks the herd.

The voice of the herd will still ring within you. And when you say: 'We have no longer the same conscience, you and I', it will be a lament and a grief.

For see, it is still this same conscience that causes your grief:

and the last glimmer of this conscience still glows in your affliction.

But do you want to go the way of your affliction, which is the way to yourself? If so, show me your strength for it and your right to it!

Are you a new strength and a new right? A first motion? A self-propelling wheel? Can you also compel stars to revolve about you?

Alas, there is so much lusting for eminence! There is so much convulsion of the ambitious! Show me that you are not one of the lustful or ambitious!

Alas, there are so many great ideas that do no more than a bellows: they inflate and make emptier.

Do you call yourself free? I want to hear your ruling idea, and not that you have escaped from a yoke.

Are you such a man as *ought* to escape a yoke? There are many who threw off their final worth when they threw off their bondage.

Free from what? Zarathustra does not care about that! But your eye should clearly tell me: free *for* what?

Can you furnish yourself with your own good and evil and hang up your own will above yourself as a law? Can you be judge of yourself and avenger of your law?

It is terrible to be alone with the judge and avenger of one's own law. It is to be like a star thrown forth into empty space and into the icy breath of solitude.

Today you still suffer from the many, O man set apart today you still have your courage whole and your hopes.

But one day solitude will make you weary, one day you

pride will bend and your courage break. One day you will cry: 'I am alone!'

One day you will no longer see what is exalted in you; and what is base in you, you will see all too closely; your sublimity itself will make you afraid, as if it were a phantom. One day you will cry: 'Everything is false!'

There are emotions that seek to kill the solitary; if they do not succeed, well, they must die themselves! But are you capable of being a murderer?

My brother, have you ever known the word 'contempt'? And the anguish of your justice in being just to those who despise you?

You compel many to change their opinion about you; they hold that very much against you. You approached them and yet went on past them: that they will never forgive you.

You go above and beyond them: but the higher you climb, the smaller you appear to the eye of envy. And he who flies is hated most of all.

'How could you be just towards me?' – that is how you must speak – 'I choose your injustice as my portion.'

They throw injustice and dirt at the solitary: but, my brother, if you want to be a star, you must shine none the less brightly for them on that account!

And be on your guard against the good and just! They would like to crucify those who devise their own virtue – they hate the solitary.

Be on your guard, too, against holy simplicity! Everything which is not simple is unholy to it: and it, too, likes to play with fire – in this case, the fire of the snake.

And be on your guard, too, against the assaults your love makes upon you! The solitary extends his hand too quickly to anyone he meets.

To many men, you ought not to give your hand, but only your paw: and I should like it if your paw had claws, too.

But you yourself will always be the worst enemy you can encounter; you yourself lie in wait for yourself in caves and forests.

Solitary man, you are going the way to yourself! And your way leads past yourself and your seven devils!

You will be a heretic to yourself and a witch and a prophet and an evil-doer and a villain.

You must be ready to burn yourself in your own flame: how could you become new, if you had not first become ashes?

Solitary man, you are going the way of the creator: you want to create yourself a god from your seven devils!

Solitary man, you are going the way of the lover: you love yourself and for that reason you despise yourself as only lovers can despise.

The lover wants to create, because he despises! What does he know of love who has not had to despise precisely what he loved?

Go apart and be alone with your love and your creating, my brother; and justice will be slow to limp after you.

Go apart and be alone with my tears, my brother. I love him who wants to create beyond himself, and thus perishes.

Thus spoke Zarathustra.

'Why do you slink so shyly through the twilight, Zarathustra? And what are you hiding so carefully under your cloak?

'Is it a treasure someone has given you? Or a child that has been born to you? Or are you now taking the way of thieves yourself, friend of the wicked?'

Truly, my brother! (said Zarathustra) it is a treasure that has been given me: it is a little truth that I carry.

But it is as unruly as a little child, and if I do not stop its mouth it will cry too loudly.

Today as I was going my way alone, at the hour when the sun sets, a little old woman encountered me and spoke thus to my soul:

'Zarathustra has spoken much to us women, too, but he has never spoken to us about woman.'

And I answered her: 'One should speak about women only to men.'

'Speak to me too of women,' she said; 'I am old enough soon to forget it.'

And I obliged the little old woman and spoke to her thus:

Everything about woman is a riddle, and everything about woman has one solution: it is called pregnancy.

For the woman, the man is a means: the end is always the child. But what is the woman for the man?

The true man wants two things: danger and play. For that reason he wants woman, as the most dangerous plaything.

Man should be trained for war and woman for the re-creation of the warrior: all else is folly.

The warrior does not like fruit that is too sweet. Therefore he likes woman; even the sweetest woman is still bitter.

Woman understands children better than a man, but man is more childlike than woman.

A child is concealed in the true man: it wants to play. Come, women, discover the child in man!

Let woman be a plaything, pure and fine like a precious stone illumined by the virtues of a world that does not yet exist.

Let the flash of a star glitter in your love! Let your hope be: 'May I bear the Superman!'

Let there be bravery in your love! With your love you should attack him who inspires you with fear.

Let your honour be in your love! Woman has understood little otherwise about honour. But let this be your honour: always to love more than you are loved and never to be second in this.

Let man fear woman when she loves. Then she bears every sacrifice and every other thing she accounts valueless.

Let man fear woman when she hates: for man is at the bottom of his soul only wicked, but woman is base.

Whom does woman hate most? – Thus spoke the iron to the magnet: 'I hate you most, because you attract me, but are not strong enough to draw me towards you.'

The man's happiness is: I will. The woman's happiness is: He will.

'Behold, now the world has become perfect!' – thus thinks every woman when she obeys with all her love.

And woman has to obey and find a depth for her surface. Woman's nature is surface, a changeable, stormy film upon shallow waters.

But a man's nature is deep, its torrent roars in subterranean caves: woman senses its power but does not comprehend it.

Then the little old woman answered me: 'Zarathustra has said many nice things, especially for those who are young enough for them.

'It is strange, Zarathustra knows little of women and yet he is right about them! Is this because with women nothing is impossible?

'And now accept as thanks a little truth! I am certainly old enough for it!

'Wrap it up and stop its mouth: otherwise it will cry too loudly, this little truth!'

'Give me your little truth, woman!' I said. And thus spoke the little old woman:

'Are you visiting women? Do not forget your whip!'

Thus spoke Zarathustra.

OF THE ADDER'S BITE

ONE day Zarathustra had fallen asleep under a fig tree because of the heat, and had laid his arms over his face. An adder came along and bit him in the neck, so that Zarathustra cried out in pain. When he had taken his arm from his face he regarded the snake: it recognized Zarathustra's eyes, turned away awkwardly and was about to go. 'No, don't go,' said Zarathustra; 'you have not received my thanks! You have awakened me at the right time, I still have a long way to go.' 'You have only a short way to go,' said the adder sadly, 'my poison is deadly.' Zarathustra smiled. 'When did a dragon ever die from the poison of a snake?' he said. 'But take your poison back! You are not rich enough to give it me!' Then the adder fell upon his neck again and licked his wound.

When Zarathustra once told this to his disciples, they asked: 'And what, O Zarathustra, is the moral of your story?' Zarathustra answered the question thus:

The good and just call me the destroyer of morals: my story is immoral.

When, however, you have an enemy, do not requite him good for evil: for that would make him ashamed. But prove that he has done something good to you.

Better to be angry than make ashamed! And when you are cursed, I do not like it that you then want to bless. Rather curse back a little!

And should a great injustice be done you, then quickly do five little injustices besides. He who bears injustice alone is terrible to behold.

Did you know this already? Shared injustice is half justice. And he who can bear it should take the injustice upon himself.

A little revenge is more human than no revenge at all. And if the punishment be not also a right and an honour for the transgressor, then I do not like your punishment.

It is more noble to declare yourself wrong than to maintain

you are right, especially when you *are* right. Only you must be rich enough for it.

I do not like your cold justice; and from the eye of your judges there always gazes only the executioner and his cold steel.

Tell me, where is the justice which is love with seeing eyes to be found?

Then devise the love that bears not only all punishment but also all guilt!

Then devise the justice that acquits everyone except the judges!

Will you learn this, too? To him who wants to be just from the very heart even a lie becomes philanthropy.

But how could I be just from the very heart? How can I give everyone what is his? Let this suffice me: I give everyone what is mine.

Finally, my brothers, guard yourselves against doing wrong to any hermit! How could a hermit forget? How could he requite?

A hermit is like a deep well. It is easy to throw a stone into it; but if it sink to the bottom, tell me, who shall fetch it out again?

Guard yourselves against offending the hermit! But if you have done so, well then, kill him as well!

Thus spoke Zarathustra.

OF MARRIAGE AND CHILDREN

I HAVE a question for you alone, my brother: I throw this question like a plummet into your soul, to discover how deep it is.

You are young and desire marriage and children. But I ask you: are you a man who *ought* to desire a child?

Are you the victor, the self-conqueror, the ruler of your senses, the lord of your virtues? Thus I ask you.

Or do the animal and necessity speak from your desire? Or isolation? Or disharmony with yourself?

I would have your victory and your freedom long for a child. You should build living memorials to your victory and your liberation.

You should build beyond yourself. But first you must be built yourself, square-built in body and soul.

You should propagate yourself not only forward, but upward! May the garden of marriage help you to do it!

You should create a higher body, a first motion, a self-propelling wheel – you should create a creator.

Marriage: that I call the will of two to create the one who is more than those who created it. Reverence before one another, as before the willers of such a will – that I call marriage.

Let this be the meaning and the truth of your marriage. But that which the many-too-many, the superfluous, call marriage – ah, what shall I call it?

Ah, this poverty of soul in partnership! Ah, this filth of soul in partnership! Ah, this miserable ease in partnership!

All this they call marriage; and they say their marriages are made in Heaven.

Well, I do not like it, this Heaven of the superfluous! No, I do not like them, these animals caught in the heavenly net!

And let the God who limps hither to bless what he has not joined stay far from me!

Do not laugh at such marriages! What child has not had reason to weep over its parents?

This man seemed to me worthy and ripe for the meaning of the earth: but when I saw his wife the earth seemed to me a house for the nonsensical.

Yes, I wish that the earth shook with convulsions when a saint and a goose mate together.

This man set forth like a hero in quest of truth and at last he captured a little dressed-up lie. He calls it his marriage.

That man used to be reserved in his dealings and fastidious in his choice. But all at once he spoilt his company once and for all: he calls it his marriage.

That man sought a handmaiden with the virtues of an angel. But all at once he became the handmaiden of a woman, and now he needs to become an angel too.

I have found all buyers cautious, and all of them have astute eyes. But even the most astute man buys his wife while she is still wrapped.

Many brief follies – that is called love with you. And your marriage makes an end of many brief follies with one long stupidity.

Your love for woman and woman's love for man: ah, if only it were pity for suffering and veiled gods! But generally two animals sense one another.

But even your best love too is only a passionate impersonation and a painful ardour. It is a torch which should light your way to higher paths.

One day you shall love beyond yourselves! So first *learn* to love! For that you have had to drink the bitter cup of your love.

There is bitterness in the cup of even the best love: thus it arouses longing for the Superman, thus it arouses thirst in you, the creator!

A creator's thirst, arrow, and longing for the Superman: speak, my brother, is this your will to marriage?

I call holy such a will and such a marriage.

Thus spoke Zarathustra.

OF VOLUNTARY DEATH

MANY die too late and some die too early. Still the doctrine sounds strange: 'Die at the right time.'

Die at the right time: thus Zarathustra teaches.

To be sure, he who never lived at the right time could hardly die at the right time! Better if he were never to be born! – Thus I advise the superfluous.

But even the superfluous make a great thing of their dying; yes, even the hollowest nut wants to be cracked.

Everyone treats death as an important matter: but as yet death is not a festival. As yet, men have not learned to consecrate the fairest festivals.

I shall show you the consummating death, which shall be a spur and a promise to the living.

The man consummating his life dies his death triumphantly, surrounded by men filled with hope and making solemn vows.

Thus one should learn to die; and there should be no festivals at which such a dying man does not consecrate the oaths of the living!

To die thus is the best death: but the second best is: to die in battle and to squander a great soul.

But equally hateful to the fighter as to the victor is your grinning death, which comes creeping up like a thief – and yet comes as master.

I commend to you my sort of death, voluntary death that comes to me because *I* wish it.

And when shall I wish it? – He who has a goal and an heir wants death at the time most favourable to his goal and his heir.

And out of reverence for his goal and his heir he will hang up no more withered wreaths in the sanctuary of life.

Truly, I do not want to be like the rope-makers: they spin out their yarn and as a result continually go backwards themselves.

Many a one grows too old even for his truths and victories; a toothless mouth has no longer the right to every truth.

And everyone who wants glory must take leave of honour in good time and practise the difficult art of – going at the right time.

One must stop permitting oneself to be eaten when one tastes best: this is understood by those who want to be loved long.

To be sure, there are sour apples whose fate is to wait until the last day of autumn: and they become at the same time ripe, yellow, and shrivelled.

In some the heart ages first and in others the spirit. And some are old in their youth: but those who are young late stay young long.

For many a man, life is a failure: a poison-worm eats at his heart. So let him see to it that his death is all the more a success.

Many a man never becomes sweet, he rots even in the summer. It is cowardice that keeps him fastened to his branch.

Many too many live and they hang on their branches much too long. I wish a storm would come and shake all this rottenness and worm-eatenness from the tree!

I wish preachers of *speedy* death would come! They would be the fitting storm and shakers of the trees of life! But I hear preached only slow death and patience with all 'earthly things'.

Ah, do you preach patience with earthly things? It is these earthly things that have too much patience with you, you blasphemers!

Truly, too early died that Hebrew whom the preachers of slow death honour: and that he died too early has since been a fatality for many.

As yet he knew only tears and the melancholy of the Hebrews, together with the hatred of the good and just – the Hebrew Jesus: then he was seized by the longing for death.

Had he only remained in the desert and far from the good and just! Perhaps he would have learned to live and learned to love the earth – and laughter as well!

Believe it, my brothers! He died too early; he himself would have recanted his teaching had he lived to my age! He was noble enough to recant!

But he was still immature. The youth loves immaturely and immaturely too he hates man and the earth. His heart and the wings of his spirit are still bound and heavy.

But there is more child in the man than in the youth, and less melancholy: he has a better understanding of life and death.

Free for death and free in death, one who solemnly says No when there is no longer time for Yes: thus he understands life and death.

That your death may not be a blasphemy against man and the earth, my friends: that is what I beg from the honey of your soul.

In your death, your spirit and your virtue should still glow like a sunset glow around the earth: otherwise yours is a bad death.

Thus I want to die myself, that you friends may love the earth more for my sake; and I want to become earth again, that I may have peace in her who bore me.

Truly, Zarathustra had a goal, he threw his ball: now may you friends be the heirs of my goal, I throw the golden ball to you.

But best of all I like to see you, too, throwing on the golden ball, my friends! So I shall stay on earth a little longer: forgive me for it!

Thus spoke Zarathustra.

I

WHEN Zarathustra had taken leave of the town to which his heart was attached and which was called The Pied Cow there followed him many who called themselves his disciples and escorted him. Thus they came to a cross-road: there Zarathustra told them that from then on he wanted to go alone: for he was a friend of going-alone. But his disciples handed him in farewell a staff, upon the golden haft of which a serpent was coiled about a sun. Zarathustra was delighted with the staff and leaned upon it; then he spoke thus to his disciples:

Tell me: how did gold come to have the highest value? Because it is uncommon and useless and shining and mellow in lustre; it always bestows itself.

Only as an image of the highest virtue did gold come to have the highest value. Gold-like gleams the glance of the giver. Gold-lustre makes peace between moon and sun.

The highest virtue is uncommon and useless, it is shining and mellow in lustre: the highest virtue is a bestowing virtue.

Truly, I divine you well, my disciples, you aspire to the bestowing virtue, as I do. What could you have in common with cats and wolves?

You thirst to become sacrifices and gifts yourselves; and that is why you thirst to heap up all riches in your soul.

Your soul aspires insatiably after treasures and jewels, because your virtue is insatiable in wanting to give.

You compel all things to come to you and into you, that they may flow back from your fountain as gifts of your love.

Truly, such a bestowing love must become a thief of all values; but I call this selfishness healthy and holy.

There is another selfishness, an all-too-poor, a hungry selfishness that always wants to steal, that selfishness of the sick, the sick selfishness.

It looks with the eye of a thief upon all lustrous things; with the greed of hunger it measures him who has plenty to eat; and it is always skulking about the table of the givers.

Sickness speaks from such craving, and hidden degeneration; the thieving greed of this longing speaks of a sick body.

Tell me, my brothers: what do we account bad and the worst of all? Is it not *degeneration*? – And we always suspect degeneration where the bestowing soul is lacking.

Our way is upward, from the species across to the super-species. But the degenerate mind which says 'All for me' is a horror to us.

Our mind flies upward: thus it is an image of our bodies, an image of an advance and elevation.

The names of the virtues are such images of advances and elevations.

Thus the body goes through history, evolving and battling. And the spirit – what is it to the body? The herald, companion, and echo of its battles and victories.

All names of good and evil are images: they do not speak out, they only hint. He is a fool who seeks knowledge from them.

Whenever your spirit wants to speak in images, pay heed; for that is when your virtue has its origin and beginning.

Then your body is elevated and risen up; it enraptures the spirit with its joy, that it may become creator and evaluator and lover and benefactor of all things.

When your heart surges broad and full like a river, a blessing and a danger to those who live nearby: that is when your virtue has its origin and beginning.

When you are exalted above praise and blame, and your will wants to command all things as the will of a lover: that is when your virtue has its origin and beginning.

When you despise the soft bed and what is pleasant and cannot make your bed too far away from the soft-hearted: that is when your virtue has its origin and beginning.

When you are the willers of a single will, and you call this dispeller of need your essential and necessity: that is when your virtue has its origin and beginning.

Truly, it is a new good and evil! Truly, a new roaring in the depths and the voice of a new fountain!

It is power, this new virtue; it is a ruling idea, and around it a subtle soul: a golden sun, and around it the serpent of knowledge.

2

Here Zarathustra fell silent a while and regarded his disciple lovingly. Then he went on speaking thus, and his voice was different:

Stay loyal to the earth, my brothers, with the power of your virtue! May your bestowing love and your knowledge serve towards the meaning of the earth! Thus I beg and entreat you.

Do not let it fly away from the things of earth and beat with its wings against the eternal walls! Alas, there has always been much virtue that has flown away!

Lead, as I do, the flown-away virtue back to earth – yes, back to the body and life: that it may give the earth its meaning, a human meaning!

A hundred times hitherto has spirit as well as virtue flown away and blundered. Alas, all this illusion and blundering still dwells in our bodies: it has there become body and will.

A hundred times has spirit as well as virtue experimented and gone astray. Yes, man was an experiment. Alas, much ignorance and error has become body in us!

Not only the reason of millennia – the madness of millennia too breaks out in us. It is dangerous to be an heir.

We are still fighting step by step with the giant Chance, and hitherto the senseless, the meaningless, has still ruled over mankind.

May your spirit and your virtue serve the meaning of the earth, my brothers: and may the value of all things be fixed anew by you. To that end you should be fighters! To that end you should be creators!

The body purifies itself through knowledge; experimenting

with knowledge it elevates itself; to the discerning man all instincts are holy; the soul of the elevated man grows joyful.

Physician, heal yourself: thus you will heal your patient too. Let his best healing-aid be to see with his own eyes him who makes himself well.

There are a thousand paths that have never yet been trodden, a thousand forms of health and hidden islands of life. Man and man's earth are still unexhausted and undiscovered.

Watch and listen, you solitaries! From the future come winds with a stealthy flapping of wings; and good tidings go out to delicate ears.

You solitaries of today, you who have seceded from society, you shall one day be a people: from you, who have chosen out yourselves, shall a chosen people spring – and from this chosen people, the Superman.

Truly, the earth shall yet become a house of healing! And already a new odour floats about it, an odour that brings health – and a new hope!

3

When Zarathustra had said these words he paused like one who has not said his last word; long he balanced the staff doubtful in his hand. At last he spoke thus, and his voice was different:

I now go away alone, my disciples! You too now go away and be alone! So I will have it.

Truly, I advise you: go away from me and guard yourselves against Zarathustra! And better still: be ashamed of him! Perhaps he has deceived you.

The man of knowledge must be able not only to love his enemies but also to hate his friends.

One repays a teacher badly if one remains only a pupil. And why, then, should you not pluck at my laurels?

You respect me; but how if one day your respect should tumble? Take care that a falling statue does not strike you dead!

You say you believe in Zarathustra? But of what importance is Zarathustra? You are my believers: but of what importance are all believers?

You had not yet sought yourselves when you found me. Thus do all believers; therefore all belief is of so little account.

Now I bid you lose me and find yourselves; and only when you have all denied me will I return to you.

Truly, with other eyes, my brothers, I shall then seek my lost ones; with another love I shall then love you.

And once more you shall have become my friends and children of one hope: and then I will be with you a third time, that I may celebrate the great noontide with you.

And this is the great noontide: it is when man stands at the middle of his course between animal and Superman and celebrates his journey to the evening as his highest hope: for it is the journey to a new morning.

Then man, going under, will bless himself; for he will be going over to Superman; and the sun of his knowledge will stand at noontide.

'*All gods are dead: now we want the Superman to live*' – let this be our last will one day at the great noontide!

Thus spoke Zarathustra.

For complete information about books available from Penguin and how to order them, please write to us at the appropriate address below. Please note that for copyright reasons the selection of books varies from country to country.

IN THE UNITED KINGDOM: Please write to *Dept. EP, Penguin Books Ltd, Bath Road, Harmondsworth, Middlesex UB7 0DA*.

IN THE UNITED STATES: Please write to *Consumer Sales, Penguin USA, P.O. Box 999, Dept. 17109, Bergenfield, New Jersey 07621-0120*. VISA and MasterCard holders call 1-800-253-6476 to order Penguin titles.

IN CANADA: Please write to *Penguin Books Canada Ltd, 10 Alcorn Avenue, Suite 300, Toronto, Ontario M4V 3B2*.

IN AUSTRALIA: Please write to *Penguin Books Australia Ltd, P.O. Box 257, Ringwood, Victoria 3134*.

IN NEW ZEALAND: Please write to *Penguin Books (NZ) Ltd, Private Bag 102902, North Shore Mail Centre, Auckland 10*.

IN INDIA: Please write to *Penguin Books India Pvt Ltd, 706 Eros Apartments, 56 Nehru Place, New Delhi 110 019*.

IN THE NETHERLANDS: Please write to *Penguin Books Netherlands bv, Postbus 3507, NL-1001 AH Amsterdam*.

IN GERMANY: Please write to *Penguin Books Deutschland GmbH, Metzlerstrasse 26, 60594 Frankfurt am Main*.

IN SPAIN: Please write to *Penguin Books S. A., Bravo Murillo 19, 1º B, 28015 Madrid*.

IN ITALY: Please write to *Penguin Italia s.r.l., Via Felice Casati 20, I-20124 Milano*.

IN FRANCE: Please write to *Penguin France S. A., 17 rue Lejeune, F-31000 Toulouse*.

IN JAPAN: Please write to *Penguin Books Japan, Ishikiribashi Building, 2-5-4, Suido, Bunkyo-ku, Tokyo 112*.

IN GREECE: Please write to *Penguin Hellas Ltd, Dimocritou 3, GR-106 71 Athens*.

IN SOUTH AFRICA: Please write to *Longman Penguin Southern Africa (Pty) Ltd, Private Bag X08, Bertsham 2013*.